Emotional Intelligence Mastery

Why EQ Can Often Matter More Than IQ

James L. Austin

Introduction

"A man who conquers himself is greater than one who conquers a thousand men in battle."
Buddha

I want to thank you for getting the book, **_Emotional Intelligence Mastery: Why EQ can Often Matter More Than IQ._**

Emotional intelligence is our ability to be aware of, control, and express one's emotions, and to handle interpersonal relationships judiciously and empathetically.

EQ is often a neglected part of our education, yet it may just have one of the most influential impacts on the success of our lives. By learning to master ourselves and then developing our awareness of the outside world, we gain the ability to change it.

I have always been a great believer that we create the life we live. Throughout my own life, I have always worked exceptionally hard to enhance my natural abilities. About six or seven years ago I realized that although academically I was above average, I lacked skills and knowledge in an important area of my life. I stumbled upon the concept of emotional intelligence, and I discovered how important it actually was.

I noticed that this was a big problem for many people that seemed to only increase the higher someone's IQ was.

Despite being relatively intelligent from a young age, I still remember a couple of times in my life when I would walk into an exam hall and sit down only to open the paper and realize that my mind had gone completely blank. At the time I thought it was because I hadn't learned the information well enough. However, as time went by I began to realize that I lacked the ability to control or regulate my emotions at crucial times and that they had the ability to cripple my performance. The problem was an emotional override of my logical brain.

Another problem I faced which is crucial to emotional intelligence, was my people skills and my ability to pick up social cues. I struggled to be able to interpret what all these inputs actually mean. I remember I lacked the knowledge of such things as simple as knowing the importance of eye contact, in Western culture, when you are talking to someone. This knowledge seemed obvious, but there I was completely oblivious to it.

Because of all of this, I decided it was in my present and future interest to find out more about this concept and to develop it. I learned through a process of trial and error of what works and what didn't for me. I found some methods for regulating my emotions worked great sometimes and were ineffective at other times. This stressed to me the importance of having a couple of tricks up my sleeve.

Through my development of EQ, I had taken this area of my life from being one of my main weaknesses to being my greatest strength. I will show you how to do the same and how to develop your EQ to enhance your life.

Thanks again for getting this book, I hope you enjoy it.

James L. Austin

© Copyright 2014 by _____ - All rights reserved.

This document is geared towards providing exact and reliable information in regards to the topic and issue covered. The publication is sold on the idea that the publisher is not required to render accounting, officially permitted, or otherwise, qualified services. If advice is necessary, legal or professional, a practiced individual in the profession should be ordered.

- From a Declaration of Principles which was accepted and approved equally by a Committee of the American Bar Association and a Committee of Publishers and Associations.

In no way is it legal to reproduce, duplicate, or transmit any part of this document by either electronic means or in printed format. Recording of this publication is strictly prohibited, and any storage of this document is not allowed unless with written permission from the publisher. All rights reserved.

The information provided herein is stated to be truthful and consistent, in that any liability, regarding inattention or otherwise, by any usage or abuse of any policies, processes, or directions contained within is the solitary and utter responsibility of the recipient reader. Under no circumstances will any legal responsibility or blame be held against the publisher for any reparation, damages, or monetary loss due to the information herein, either directly or indirectly.

Respective authors own all copyrights not held by the publisher.

James L. Austin

The information herein is offered for informational purposes solely and is universal as so. The presentation of the information is without a contract or any guarantee assurance.

The trademarks that are used are without any consent, and the publication of the trademark is without permission or backing by the trademark owner. All trademarks and brands within this book are for clarifying purposes only and are the owned by the owners themselves, not affiliated with this document.

Contents

Introduction

Chapter 1- Why Is EQ So Important For Success

Chapter 2-The Four Areas of Emotional Intelligence And Why They Matter

Chapter3-Developing Emotional Awareness

Chapter 4-Harnessing The Power Of Emotional Management

Chapter 5- Learning How To Read People And Grasping Social Awareness

Chapter 6-Relationship Management

Conclusion

James L. Austin

Why Is EQ So Important For Success

In our society, there is such a large emphasis on IQ as a measure of the success we're likely to achieve. This presumption is often very limited. A high IQ doesn't guarantee success in life alone; it has to be used alongside other important attributes so that you can be able to apply the right leverage, at the right time, to produce the desired result. Often it is the other attributes that turn out to be the most important contributing factors.

Emotional Intelligence is one of these factors. Our "EQ" allows us to assess a situation, think clearly, motivate ourselves, connect with others and much more. It is a crucial building block to success in life.

To understand how EQ matters for success we must understand the inner workings of our brain. One part of the brain which we will call the "lizard brain," is completely ruled and dictated by our emotions and primal urges. This part of the brain is called the Amygdala; it is responsible for fear, anger, and negativity. Animals such as lizards or chickens have this very primal brain. We developed this part of our brain very early in the stages of human evolution and have since developed other parts of the brain on top of this to aid in our higher thinking. Our lizard brain has a very important role though as it keeps us alive; it triggers a fight or flight response to danger, it gives us the urge to eat, and to reproduce. When the fight or flight response is triggered, blood is diverted away from the brain to the major muscles in order to prime them to move. The hormones Adrenaline and Cortisol are released into our bloodstream, elevating our heart rate, and changing the way we breathe. Our logical brains become hijacked by our primal survival mechanisms. This is very useful and it does keep us safe. The problem though, is our brains struggle to distinguish between real danger and perceived fear of failure. Furthermore, we have the added obstacle that it is our higher brain function and logical part of our brain which is the very resource we may need to help us in that moment. This part of the brain then struggles to help us as it is being hijacked and overruled by our lizard brain.

Our Lizard brain also gets in the way of our success by creating resistance to completing our goals. It is the reason why we procrastinate instead of doing what we need to do in order to grow. It is why we do not follow through with ideas and why we are so afraid of failure. Simply put this part of the brain is designed to minimize risk in order to maximize safety. It wants us to keep doing what we are already doing and it has a "If you're not dead yet, don't change anything" mentality. From an evolutionary point of view, altering our habits increases our risk of death. Even something such as rising through the ranks in our tribe from a survival standpoint could increase the danger in our lives.

These primal psychological driving forces are continually influencing us in ways such as fear of failure and even fear of success. They create resistance towards doing what we know we should do. As Stephen Pressfield said "Like a magnetized needle floating on a surface of the oil, resistance will unfailingly point to true North. Meaning that calling or action it most wants to stop us from doing. We can use this. We can use it as a compass. We can navigate by resistance, letting it guide us to that calling or action that we must follow before all others." Our lizard brain will stop us from going after what we want and will stop us from succeeding if we let it. We must learn to counteract this and tame this part of the brain. This can be done through grasping a control over our emotions and an awareness on how we are being influenced by them.

How your emotions significantly affect your judgment

Another way in which our emotions affect our lives is their ability to distort our decision-making abilities. Our emotions affect our decision-making in quite a significant way. In 1983, Johnson and Tversky studied the effect of how incidental emotions affect our decision-making. It was the first empirical demonstration to show the effects of our emotional state on our ability to make decisions. In the study, the participants were asked to read newspaper stories which were designed to give each of them either a positive or negative emotional impact. They were then asked to estimate certain fatality frequencies for different causes of death. The participants who read the positive stories estimated much more optimistic estimates for the fatality frequencies. Whereas, the people primed with the negative stories, gave more pessimistic estimates. The surprising thing about this study was that the effect of mood on the judgment didn't depend on the content of the subsequent judgments or the content of the stories. It was just affected by the mood of the stories in general. This shows us that something as simple as reading an unrelated story in a newspaper can alter the decisions we make.

When emotions cloud our judgments, we can be prone to making foolish mistakes. Even when we believe we are thinking rationally, our outlook can be extremely skewed. What if your emotions were currently clouding your judgment? It would be in your best interest to learn to become aware of the emotional driving forces affecting you. Furthermore, it would be of the utmost importance to learn how to train your mind to think from a clear headspace.

Mirror neurons and our ability to connect with others

How we connect and communicate with others is another link in the chain of emotional intelligence. Our ability to make connections with people is vital for our success in life. Becoming a person who can easily make friends can smooth out difficulties in our lives. Sales statistics not only show us someone is more likely to buy a product if they like the person selling it, but actually that they are often willing to pay more for a product if they like the person.

Our ability to connect does not only help our work life, but it is also the foundation of our happiness. The Harvard Study of Adult Development has been running for over 75 years and has tracked the lives of 724 men, many of whom are now deceased. The study took two groups of men and continuously followed up with them asking about their lives. One group started when they were sophomores in college, and the other group was one that consisted of boys who were from Boston's poorest areas. After 75 years of research, what they found was that the men's happiness was directly correlated with the quality of relationships they had in their lives. They also found that good relationships not only make us happier, but also keep us healthier and allow us to live longer. By learning to connect with people and have quality relationships we gain the knowledge to be happier, healthier, and more successful.

What allows us to feel empathy?
In the 90's in Parma Italy, a group of researchers were studying the part of the brain known as the motor cortex. This is the part of the brain in charge of processing action and movement. You would activate this part of the brain, for example, if you were to use your hand to pick something up. The researchers were studying single cells in the motor cortex by inserting highly sensitive sensors into this part of a monkey's brain. Part of the analysis of the sensor was sent to a speaker. The speaker would then make a bleep when the neurons in the monkey's motor cortex were firing. So every time the monkey moved the speaker would bleep.

One sunny day, one of the researchers walk into the lab with an ice-cream in his hand. As the researcher is eating his ice-cream, he hears a bleep in the background. He looks at the monkey, and it is not moving. He lifts his arm up once more to get another lick of the ice cream and he hears the bleep again. He had been watching the monkey the whole time and it had not moved. The monkey was not performing any action, yet the neurons in the motor cortex were firing.

This anomaly then led to a revolution of how we perceive the brain. The neurons in the monkey's brain were firing as it watched someone else's action. Scientists then started researching what is now known as mirror neurons. These are neurons that fire because of other people's actions. Scientists developed their knowledge of these neurons to uncover that they even fire when understanding the goal of the other person's actions.

In addition to this discovery, it was also found that mirror neurons are experience dependent. This means if you know an action well, these neurons are more likely to fire when you see others performing that action. So a soccer player's mirror neurons will more likely start to fire when watching a soccer game rather than a person who has never played the sport.

Research was carried out in a study where the subjects were asked to watch a video of basketball players trying to throw the basketball into the net. The videos were paused at different times and the subjects were asked to predict whether the shot went into the net or not.

It was found that normal subjects and even expert sports writers needed to watch both the manual action of the player's movement and also had to watch the ball travel some distance through the air in order to accurately predict the outcome.

Experienced basketball players were then asked to perform the same test, but they only needed to see the manual action of the player to accurately predict the result. This helps show us one reason why we may have mirror neurons. They can be used to anticipate and understand goals, intentions, and their subsequent results. Our brain uses these to be able to pick up on emotional states of other people and develop a sense of their intentions. Our mirror neurons help us to develop our social intuition.

Can EQ be developed and what is its effect on salary?

EQ is almost completely derived from the environment that we have grown up in. It is a result of nurture being dominant over nature. We are very social animals and in the early stages of human evolution it was essential for us to communicate and have strong social skills with the other members of our tribe. Our mirror neurons gave us these abilities, but the extent to which we use them is mostly dependent on our life experience

Since our social intuition is heavily dependent on the environment we have grown up in so far, it means that we can develop this intuition. It is a flexible skill that can be learned. Unlike IQ, we can drastically increase our EQ in a relatively short period of time. All we have to do is enhance our knowledge and hone our skills.

A substantial reason for developing our skills in this area would be the financial incentives. According to Dr. Travis Bradberry and Nick Tassler, EQ has a significant effect on the annual salary you are likely to achieve. They tested over 42,000 people on their emotional intelligence. They then compared their scores to the people's annual income. The results showed that people with high EQs make on average $29,000 more per year than those people with low EQs. The relationship is directly proportional and an increase in EQ directs you towards an increase in income.

James L. Austin

The Four Areas of Emotional Intelligence And Why They Matter

Emotional intelligence has four key areas:

- Emotional Awareness
- Emotional Management
- Social Awareness
- Relationship Management

These areas all intertwine with each other, but I recommend focusing on one area at a time in order to get the most out of the book.

Emotional Awareness is our ability to recognize our emotions and understand their causes.

So before we deal with a problem, we must become aware that there is one. A computer becomes self-aware when it knows it's a computer. When we realize we are in an emotional state and that it could be affecting our judgment we become emotionally self-aware. This means we gain knowledge of ourselves. We can acknowledge our weaknesses and potential emotional blind spots. When we become aware that we are emotionally affected it can help to differentiate between our emotions by labeling them accurately. For example, do you know the difference between envy and jealousy? The answer is, that jealousy is involved within relationships and envy is not. Simple labeling such as this can be significant when dealing with the problem.

Once we have become aware of an emotion, we must then dig deeper into its meaning. Often when we experience an emotion, we fail to investigate and find the root cause of it. If we do not understand our emotions it becomes more difficult to deal with them.

Qualities of someone with good emotional awareness:

- You can register when you are in an emotional state and you realize that it could be affecting your judgment.
- You understand why you are feeling what you are feeling

- You know what triggers emotional reactions within yourself and you know how to avoid them.

Emotional Management is how we deal with our emotions. Our emotions are never the result of an event, but rather our perception of how that event influences us. We can choose to feel differently once we acquire the knowledge to do so. Emotional management is not about training ourselves to be happy twenty-four hours a day, seven days a week. It is about learning to balance our emotions and having the power to quickly change our emotional state if need be. Our emotions serve very significant purposes to us. Without them, we wouldn't have any reason to do anything. Even the depths of our sadness can catalyze our creativity, our anger can fuel our motivation, and our regret can help imprint important lessons that we must learn into our subconscious. All emotions are useful and serve a purpose. However, the problem is that they can override our logical minds at inappropriate times as well. So we must learn to become aware and then deal with this problem.

Qualities of someone with good emotional management:

- You do not lash out emotionally.

- You can change your emotional state quickly if need be.

- You can engage different emotions at certain times that will benefit you.

- You have the knowledge to know how to motivate yourself.

Social Awareness is your ability to realize other's feelings, needs and concerns and to judge the environment and its etiquette. It is the skill of empathy, which is being able to see the world as though through the eyes of another.

Qualities of someone with good social awareness:

- You can empathize to how others feel.
- You are good at noticing social and behavioral cues.
- You can listen and understand the deeper meaning behind someone's words.
- You have the knowledge that more than one person can be right at the same time.

Relationship Management is how you handle the relationships in your life using your knowledge of the previous three elements of EQ. It is our ability to influence, lead, develop other's abilities, create change, manage conflict, build bonds and to create effective teamwork/collaboration.

Qualities of someone with good relationship management:

- You get on well with people.
- You are a person others feel they can trust.
- You are an effective leader.
- You are upfront and honest in your relationships in a respectful way.
- People feel valued by you.

James L. Austin

Developing Emotional Awareness

Emotional awareness is crucial for all aspects of emotional intelligence. It is the foundational skill. Even knowing that this concept exists could have already raised your awareness. Before now, it was probably something you never even considered to take into account. Without an accurate awareness of our emotions, our decision-making abilities are compromised.

I once read somewhere that the average millionaire had made ten thousand good decisions to get to where they are. I don't know how accurate this is, nevertheless, I believe the point still stands. Decision making is very important for success and because of this, it is important to become aware of our emotional influences and the bias they create.

Professor Bracket who is the director of the Yale Centre for Emotional Intelligence performed a study on teachers. The researchers firstly primed the teacher's emotional state by asking them to think of a good or a bad day. Once the teachers were in this slightly altered emotional state, they were then asked to grade Middle School essays.

What the researchers found was that there was one to two grade differences among the teachers who were asked about a good day and positively primed and those who were asked about a bad day to negatively prime them. These results were as expected due to the extensive research that had already been performed on this topic. What was unusual, however, was the answers that the researchers got when they asked the teachers if they thought that their emotional state affected their marking. Ninety percent of the teachers said that it in no way could have altered the grades they gave. They were certain that this could not have influenced their marking, yet the results clearly indicate that it did.

What this study tells us, is not only will we look more pessimistically at the decisions we are making in a low emotional state, but also that we are not even aware that our emotions are affecting our decision making.

Our Psychological State

There is a term used in psychology called "State". State consists of the feelings and emotions you are receiving during that time. Our brains work differently when we are in a confident state compared to an insecure/anxious state. It is similar to a journey in a car. We have our goal or intention in our brain which is like our destination in the car. When we are in a confident state it is as if there is a highway from where we are now to where we need to go. The journey is very efficient and straight forward. It becomes easier to handle problems and think up solutions. When we are in an anxious/insecure state our brains work distinctly different. It is the equivalent of travelling down rural country roads to get to your destination. There is lots of stopping, twists, turns and you may struggle to ever get there. Our mind becomes inefficient and it becomes increasingly hard to get to our destination and solve our problem. State is a road map for the neuro-pathways that our brain uses to think. It is easy when you are feeling confident, to take a challenge head on. When you feel confident, you trust that you can handle it and you get full access to your mental resources. The opposite can be said when we are anxious; our brains are restricted from working to their full capacity.

Furthermore, our memory is particularly "state access dependent". This means that our current state affects what memories we will access. When we are angry we remember all the times when we were angry. When we are sad we remember all the times we were sad. This then means that once we are in an emotional state, it can be difficult to get out of it as all of our memories of other times when we felt that way come flooding back to us. This creates a self-sustaining loop that begins to trap us in our emotional state and stops us from seeing clearly. Our emotions thus have the power to warp the reality we perceive around us.

You're not you when you're hungry

There was a famous series of candy bar commercials in the UK for a candy bar called Snickers. The advertisement would show a well-dressed diva in an everyday setting. One of the co-stars in the advertisement would say "Have a Snickers," the diva would eat the candy bar and suddenly be transformed into an everyday person. The advertisement then concluded, "You're not you when you're hungry."

It is an over exaggerated example, but it gets a message across. In a very hungry state we think and act differently.

There was a famous saying about this from a judge called Jerome Frank. He said that justice was "What the judge ate for breakfast." This sounds silly when you first hear it. However, this may not be too far from the truth.

Ben Gurion studied Israeli parole hearings for 10 months. What he found was that when the judges start off their day, the percentage of people who got parole was around 65%. This then drops throughout the next couple of hours until it goes to zero. Then after lunch, something strange happens. The number jumps back up to 65% again.

The judge's decisions to give parole appears to be directly linked to their appetite. The hungrier the judge gets, the lower the percentage getting parole will be. Immediately after lunch and when their hunger is satisfied the percentage getting parole jumps up again. The judge's state is altered when they are feeling hungry. It's a scary thought to think we can be so easily swayed by something as simple as if we are hungry or not. There are so many small contributors that can make a very large change in the decisions we make. Because of this, there is an extreme importance on becoming aware of this and taking certain precautions and actions to help us think clearly and make better decisions.

Becoming aware that you're emotions have created a bias

A good indication that our decision-making abilities may be compromised is to notice, recurring negative thoughts. When we have a problem with something, the mind will usually start to replay these thoughts on repeat. It is because we are unable to accept the reality that has been presented to us. This can mean one minor event can lead to ruining an entire day. You can become unable to think of anything else. It might even stop you from getting work done or enjoying family time. The strange thing is, it is often of absolutely no benefit for us to relive something like this and it merely prolongs the pain. You should always be consciously monitoring your thoughts to see what's going on in your mind. If you notice this happening; it is time to deal with the emotion.

Using your body for awareness

Another aspect you should consciously monitor are the feelings in your body. Is your heart rate elevated or is your breathing shallow? Do you feel a tightness in your chest or sickness in your stomach? Noticing this helps to indicate to us that something may be wrong. Our emotions produce very physical symptoms that can help to make us aware of our emotional state. What's going on in our mind creates a very noticeable difference in our bodies.

Meditation also helps you to get you more in touch with the sensations in your body and the thoughts in your head. You then develop your ability to feel subtle changes in your body. It skyrockets self-awareness of our emotions. The practice creates a balanced place for self-observation and allows us to see things from a new perspective.

Sometimes our involvement blinds us

Despite our best efforts to think without bias, it is often best to double check our actions or thoughts. Seeking impartial advice can help to do this. Don't be afraid to ask for outside opinions on your actions or thoughts as long as the person is willing to be honest with you and is unbiased by the situation. They can help to show you if you are acting or thinking foolishly.

Gaining a deep awareness of ourselves

Once you have become aware of your emotional state, it's time to dive deeper into it and ask why you are you feeling this way. You can then label what the emotion is and take adequate steps to address it. Is it an action you have done that you aren't proud of? Has someone else broken some of your expectations you had for them? It is important to question these emotions.

Psychologists implement numerous methods to get down to the root cause of a problem in their patients. The "Why" method is one of these and it is simple but powerful. The psychologist just keeps asking some form of the question "Why?" At the start, you may find yourself giving mere surface level answers such as "It just is," or "Because." However, if you continue to push and keep asking why you will be able to get down to the source. Sometimes the problem will be conflicting values or expectations in your head. If you force yourself to follow this process, you will realize that there often isn't much of a problem at all but just a lack of understanding of yourself. Understanding the source of the problem is essential to finding a solution and can also help prevent it entirely.

Understanding our psychological motivators

Another building block of emotional awareness, is knowing how to motivate ourselves to achieve our goals.

Success is strongly connected to our ability to suppress temporary pleasure for a long term gain. Psychologist Walter Mischel led a series of studies in the 1960'2 and 1970's that looked at this ability and its effects on the participant's lives.

In this study, children were placed in a room and then a marshmallow was sat down in front of them. The children were told they could eat one marshmallow immediately or they could wait and get two marshmallows later on. The examiner then left the child in the room alone for approximately 15 minutes. The researchers then watched the children as they fought the urge to eat the marshmallow in front of them. Some children gave into temptation while others stayed strong and made it through the 15 minutes to claim their prize.

The study followed up with the children later on in life and monitored their S.A.T. scores. The children who delayed their gratification for a greater reward performed better on their S.A.T. scores later in life. Their ability to delay pleasure/endure temporary pain helped them achieve a more long term goal.

Putting off instant gratification is easier said than done, so often temptation can get the best of us. The idea of watching television over putting the work into our goals causes our success to take a back seat. Unluckily these extra bits of work add up in the long term. They can make all of the difference in achieving our goals.

When training our ability to delay instant gratification, it can help to get our emotions working for us instead of against us. To do this, we can alter our two main driving forces in life; pain and pleasure. If we adjust the ratio of pain to pleasure. These are our two main driving forces in life.

James L. Austin

Tasks become easier when we aware of our potential gain or loss of our actions. When we develop crystal clear knowledge of the benefits of what we are doing; the activity becomes significantly easier.

The task also becomes easier when we have a clear understanding of the pain we will receive by inaction. Once we gain knowledge of these reasons; our path becomes easier to follow.

Harnessing The Power Of Emotional Management

It is an extremely useful skill to be able to change the state we are in. Whether you are an athlete before a game or a business owner; grasping control over your emotions will give you a competitive edge and change your life.

In this section, I will show you mindsets and mental tricks that are extremely useful for changing your emotional state. I will give you an idea of the general principles behind all of them and why they work. Some of them will seem very illogical. What you must understand is that the emotional parts of the brain are very different from the logical parts. The emotional mind does not need a step by step instruction on the details of why something works. It can often be tricked into changing your emotional state through a method that logically does not make sense. I urge you to keep an open mind and to just try the techniques anyway. It can sometimes be the most illogical methods that are the most effective when it comes to changing your emotional state.

The first step after awareness

After we have become aware of the cause of our current emotional state, there are two things we can do about it:

- We can either change the cause of the emotion so that it does not happen in future.

- We can change how we view or how we feel about it.

Ideally, you want to change the cause. Unfortunately, it is not always possible to do this. If you can't change the cause; you must change how you view it.

The same event looked at from a different perspective can seem to be completely different. In some cultures, they see death as something to be celebrated, while for others it is a time of great loss. There is no clear black and white meaning of anything; everything depends on how we perceive it. When we change our perception of an event, we can choose a point of view that helps us the most.

What is it to have good luck?

There was a farmer who lived on the outskirts of a town in Asia. This farmer was slightly odd, he did things slightly different from the rest of the townspeople and he was viewed as an outsider. One day he went into town and got a brand new saddle for his horse. The farmer wakes up the following morning and to his surprise, the horse has escaped and ran off during the night. The townspeople hear about this and the next day they come out to his farm. "We're sorry to hear about your horse, it's such bad luck you have," the townspeople said. The farmer replies to them "Could be good luck, could be bad luck, I don't know." The townspeople look at him as if he is deranged and then leave. A few days later the farmer's horse returns, only now it has also brought back three wild stallions with it. The townspeople upon hearing the good news go out to the man's farm. "We heard about your horse; it's such good luck you have," the townspeople say with glee. "Could be good luck, could be bad luck, I don't know," proclaims the farmer. The townspeople storm out and call the man an "Idiot." A few days later the farmer's son is taming one of the wild stallions when suddenly it kicks back and breaks the son's leg. The townspeople rush out to the man's farm upon hearing the news. They say, "We're so sorry to hear about your son, it's such bad luck you have." The farmer replies, "It could be good luck, could be bad luck, I don't know." The townspeople have had enough after hearing this, they have come out to consolidate this man who's clearly delusional. They storm off once again into the town.

The next day a messenger rides into town. This messenger is dressed up fancier than most messengers. The townspeople gather around to listen to what this man has to say. The messenger projects his voice saying "A message from your king, the country is at war and all eligible sons older than the age of fourteen are needed for battle. You have three days to prepare." The town's people are caught off guard by the news. Their sons will be sent off to the front lines of war and quite possibly die. The sadness infects the crowd and the worry sets in.

There is only one son in the village of the right age who is not eligible to go. He has broken a leg.

It's a very old story, but the point is very clear. We have no idea the cosmic significance of events. An event that could be perceived as bad luck could be the greatest thing that has ever happened to you and vice versa. Getting caught in traffic could have stopped you being in a car crash later that day. Getting fired from your job could lead to you meeting the love of your life. We have no idea where anything leads us. Although it may be hard, we can learn to take a broader view of events and see the bigger picture.

Whatever doesn't kill you makes you stronger

Another favorable mindset to have is the "Whatever doesn't kill me makes me stronger," attitude. The harder the problems we get through; the better we become at overcoming difficulties. Discomfort is essential in our lives and without it we become weakened. With a lack of adequate exercise; our bones weaken. Business' with a lack of competition can neglect important areas that could help them to survive more difficult times. In the same way if we lack emotionally challenging events in our lives we become more easily emotionally hurt.

It is often the skills we learn in our darkest hours that are the most valuable. Becoming resilient is basically improving our emotional immune system. The more discomfort we get through; the higher the difficulties of problems we will be able to solve in the future. The problems you face and adapt to could lead you on the very path to success.

The story of Traf-O-Data

There was a startup company created by two young men in the 1970's. The company was called "Traf-O-Data", and its premise was to "Read the raw data from roadway traffic counters and create reports for the traffic engineers." The company's goal was to optimize traffic and thus end road congestion.

They launched their first product called Traf-O-Data 8008 in the 1970's. The product turned out to be a complete failure and the machine quite simply didn't work.

At the time this was a devastating blow for the two men. All their hard work and effort had appeared to have gone to waste.

Instead of accepting permanent failure, they decided to move on. The two young entrepreneurs were Paul Allen and Bill Gates. Their next venture was a company you have probably heard of called Microsoft. The company made both of them billionaires and Bill Gates went on to become the richest person on the planet.

Paul Allen later said, "Even though Traf-O-Data wasn't a roaring success, it was seminal in preparing us to make Microsoft's first product a couple of years later."

Bill and Paul's failure was a key point on their path to success and allowed them to go on and change the world.

Instead of shying away from failure and discomfort, if you instead expect it, embrace, and use it; it will make you much more emotionally resilient. This resilience will help you through the hard times in your life. As Eleanor Roosevelt said, "The stumbling block to the pessimist is the stepping stone to the optimist."

Quickly changing your emotional state

One of the greatest examples of emotional control I have ever heard of was from the motivational life coach and expert on Neuro-Linguistic Programming (NLP), Anthony Robbins. NLP is simply changing the way your brain works to get the results you want. One of the aspects of NLP involves being able to change your emotional state and emotional reactions. Tony uses this knowledge to alter his state before every speaking event to prime his mind. Five minutes before he was about to start a 5-daylong seminar event, his ability to do this was put to the test.

Tony is preparing backstage as usual for the event. He sees a man walk up to him with a dire look on his face. This man is the CEO of Tony's company and a friend. The man opens his mouth with dread and says "Your business is out of money. Three-quarters of a million dollars has been stolen. I think you should just shut down this whole thing. I'm sorry. I quit."

Tony stands there gob smacked and blown away by this news. He has five minutes before he is supposed to go on stage in front of five thousand people. It is his job to be motivating and inspiring but he is distraught. He has been told his company is bankrupt and his world has been turned upside down.

Tony still in a state of shock thinks to himself and realizes he has two options. He can cancel the show to immediately work on trying to sort this out, or he can continue with the event. The deadline is quickly approaching. The pressure is on. He must now decide what direction his company will take. Indecision, anxiety, and anger begin to take over him.

Tony realizes he is in an inappropriate state to make a decision, so he takes control over his emotions and calms himself down. From this much more leveled place, he digs down deep and decides to do the show. Tony has one ace up his sleeve. He has studied neuro-linguistic programming for years, and he knows he is a master at altering his emotional state. He knows people can feel whatever way they want at any moment if they know how.

Tony then begins to prime his emotional state to become energetic and motivating.

Minutes later he is on stage and expressing himself charismatically. Tony delivered the seminar as if he didn't have a care in the world. His emotional state of worry and anger had no benefit to him at this time, so he chose to change it.

It turned out that Tony had a crooked employee who had embezzled the money from his company. He could have wallowed in anger and regret, but he chose a better way. In the following years, he turned it all around and got his company performing better than ever.

This was a display of absolute emotional control at a time when most of us would have been paralyzed by anxiety. It proves the extent to which we can develop our EQ. Tony uses some of the techniques I will describe in the following pages.

Acceptance must come first

For our minds, the most challenging part of dealing with an emotion can often be accepting its cause. When something bad happens to us the mind denies what has happened and sends us into negative thought loops. On a conscious logical level, you know that the event has happened. You know it can no longer be changed, but emotionally your mind can't accept it. You begin to relive the event over and over in your head because of this. You just can't let go of it.

Holding onto these thoughts is of no benefit to us. It stops us from moving on and dealing with the problem.

It can also be difficult for us to accept the emotional state we find ourselves in. A prime example of this, is when we feel overwhelmed by a new environment. I know personally it can feel like I'm locked up inside my head struggling to transition into that social and outgoing mood. It is especially hard when I know I need to be charismatic in a certain situation. The ironic thing here is my sense of a need to loosen up stops me from doing so. If you are a natural introvert, you may resonate with this feeling. Acceptance is key here and it is the foundational step.

Often even talking to someone about it will trigger acceptance to that emotion. When we say it out loud, it is easier for the mind to accept that it was real. I'm not suggesting you complain to someone. This method is far more proactive and beneficial than that. When you feel overwhelmed in a social occasion, for example, you could say to someone, "This place is kind of overwhelming," then moving on to a different topic. The statement seems insignificant, but you'll find it is very effective at allowing your mind to let go of resistance. This then transitions you into acceptance and from there you can build your emotional state.

Simply writing down what has happened on paper is another useful method for acceptance. Once you have done this, you can then simply tear up the sheet. It can often be as if you are tearing up your problems. This sounds ridiculous, however, our emotional mind is not logical. I suppose it's similar to when we logically know we shouldn't be upset, yet we still are. Seeing your problems being torn up will start to satisfy this emotional part of our mind.

Another rather illogical trick to use is to learn to accept what you cannot accept. For example, if you are angry about an event that has happened to you. Start off by saying to yourself that you accept what has happened. If that doesn't work, accept that you cannot accept what has happened. After this, you may immediately feel yourself letting go of your emotional resistance. If that doesn't work, accept that you cannot accept, that you cannot accept what has happened.

Add as many of these as you need but it shouldn't take too many. Once again it may seem extremely stupid and simplistic but doing this is remarkably effective at tricking the emotional brain into acceptance. It is very useful for getting over very strong emotions such as anger.

Doing these simple tricks help the mind to let go of resistance to what has happened allowing us to move on.

Meditation

There's a reason why Fortune 500 companies like Google and Goldman Sachs are using meditation practices within their companies. Meditation is one of the most useful skills you can learn. It has so many benefits to almost all aspects of life, but I will stick to the relevant ones for this book. What meditation allows you to do is break the emotional pattern that you are in and see things from a clear, emotionally-uninterrupted viewpoint.

You will be able to see if you are acting foolishly out of your ego, if there's a different way to do something or anything else of that nature. It is the equivalent of bringing in an impartial judge to help you with your decision. A judge who has no bias and can make a good impartial decision. Our emotional state limits our mind to only seeing specific points of view or certain solutions to problems. So we must learn to address our emotional states to develop better decision-making skills. Meditation is one gateway to this, allowing us to calm down and significantly reduce our stress.

Stress is a mixture of the presence of the hormones Adrenaline and Cortisol being released into your body. This causes your body to act accordingly reinforcing your emotional state. Meditation can break this pattern, and drastically reduce the levels of these two hormones changing the way you feel. When your body feels different, it allows your mind to think differently. This allows us to begin working from a non-emotionally biased viewpoint. It breaks your negative thought loops and your train of thought allowing you to figure out other solutions and see other viewpoints. Meditation is the perfect activity for when you are struggling with a decision or you believe that you are emotionally biased.

Meditation Exercise- Mindfulness

The following exercise is a meditation you can use to clear your emotions to have clarity of thought. Keep in mind that it is like any skill, the more you practice it, the more you will get out of it. I recommend daily practice.

- Sit down in a comfortable position in a chair or with your legs crossed on the ground. Keep your back up straight and not slouched over. Get comfortable; once you begin, you won't be able to move about.

- Set an alarm for 15- 20 minutes. Make sure it will go off by itself as you are not allowed to look at the time.

- Now either choose to do it with your eyes closed or partially open, but whatever you choose, do not change.

- Now you're training yourself to be thoughtless. However, if I tell you to think of nothing, you're thinking. In the same way, if I tell you not to think of a pink elephant, you think of a pink elephant. So what you have to do instead of this is put your awareness into your breathing. Just watch as your lungs fill up and empty, pay attention to the resulting sensations in your body because of it.

- Thoughts will enter your head but just become aware of them and instead of trying not to think of them, imagine them as a cloud just floating by and then bring your awareness back to your breath. Go deep into the subtle sensations of it. Is the air you breathe out and passes your lips warmer as it goes in or out? Try to become very aware of your body in this way and notice all the little differences, just watching and observing them.

- Continue to watch your breath and simply acknowledge thoughts as they arise and let them float past before bringing your awareness back to your breathing.

Continue this process for your set time.

In this type of mindfulness meditation, you don't try and breathe in any certain way; you just accept the way the body breathes naturally and the thoughts that come into your head. If you experience an itch, focus on it fully and accept it, and it will pass. Don't judge yourself whether you can remain thoughtless or not, it is a practice of acceptance, there is no good or bad. It's all good as long as you are doing it.

You can get frustrated when you start this as it is difficult to remain thoughtless. If this happens you must remember the more you do it, the easier it becomes.

I would suggest setting a rule of meditating every day for at least 3 weeks and to do this for at least 15 minutes at a time. This will give you a grasp of the skill and allow you to notice its benefits.

If you struggle with this; you can start to use guided meditations instead. It will also help you break your thought patterns however I find it slightly less effective.

Meditation is an unbelievably useful skill and very effective at changing your emotional state and creating a clear headspace for decision making. It is also a tool that will help the development of your EQ in more ways than one.

James L. Austin

Overcoming anxiety and panic

Yet another problem we need to address, is when we hit a state of anxiety. It can completely wipe us out and catch us out on the blindside. I know myself from experience that sometimes things go wrong that can send you into panic mode. This can then be amplified if there is a time frame for you to act. The irony is that when you are in this panic mode; it is almost impossible to think of a clear solution. The fact that you know you need to act fast also increases the panic and exaggerates this effect. This continues your inaction and keeps you in this downward spiral. I think most of us have experienced this feeling and if you haven't you probably will at some stage.

When in these heightened states of panic, it can sometimes be too difficult to sit and meditate normally. In this state, we have the desire to move and do something that feels more proactive.

The first thing to do in this situation is to take back control of your body. To do this, stop and pause for a second. Stand up and take 8 deep controlled breaths. When you are breathing in, breathe the air in as though it was going down deep into your belly. Breathe as deeply as you can and fully expand your stomach.

It may feel strange to be breathing using your belly in this way, but this is the way we are designed to breathe. It allows for a much better oxygen uptake and it is the way we breathe as babies. It is only as we get older we start to breathe more from up in our chests. This method is far less efficient.

By taking 8 deep controlled belly breaths, you will be able to relax your breathing and your heart rate. It may only be a slight difference, but it will help transfer you to a calmer state.

From here you can choose which emotional management tool or tools you will employ in order to get you in a more effective state.

Meditation to heal past traumas and how to heal the mind through the body

Sometimes we can have trouble letting go of feelings or emotions from the past. We never learned to properly deal with these and thus we still carry them around with us. The upcoming exercise helps you to deal with these issues and to let finally go of them.

In the same way that when you get a massage; it helps to reduce your stress levels active meditations such as the one I describe can use your body to help heal your mind. Once again you will have to neglect logic here in order to trump the emotional parts of the mind.

When the mind experiences stress, it often stores it as tension in the muscles or as a specific reaction in the body. Often stress can be felt in the back and shoulders. By physically helping the muscles in these areas to loosen up, it's like manually pushing the stress out of the body. You cannot logically let go of these emotions you're holding on to. You cannot think your way out of them. This meditation will help you to use your body to help you to let go of what you are holding onto.

The process:

- Sit up in a chair with your spine straight, your hands on your lap and close your eyes. In the following meditation, you're going to pay attention to the sensations and tightening of specific muscles when you think or recall a certain event. You can also apply the same process if it is an event you are currently worrying about.

- Bring up the specific trauma or event in your head that you're having trouble letting go of. Notice where in the body you feel it, whether it's tingling in the stomach, tightness in the chest or whatever else you feel. Focus in on the sensation and focus on what it feels like.

- With every breath imagine your awareness lowering down to the bottom of your spine. Imagine your head's down there; your nose is down there, and you're breathing from there.

- Take a deep breath for 6 seconds through the nose (again imagining your nose and your brain are at the bottom of your spine).

- Hold for 2 seconds

- Breathe out for 6 seconds making a constant ssshhh sound (as if telling someone to be quiet).

- Hold for 2 seconds and then breathe normally for 2 seconds

Then repeat this 3 times. On the end of the 3rd time bring your awareness back to that feeling of regret, stress or anxiety in your body.

- Now, this time, I want you to perform the same process as above only when you're breathing in; imagine this uncomfortable sensation rising up through the body.
- When you breathe out; imagine you're pushing it out of your body.
- Repeat this 3 times.

You will find that after this, you will be a lot more relaxed and looser than before. If you practice this even for 2 minutes every day, you'll be amazed at how you're able to let go of these worries, anxieties, and regrets. It is also good for when you are in a state of anxiety. As discussed before, it can be hard to perform a mindfulness meditation when we feel this way. The active meditation satisfies your urge to do something proactive.

How to use your body to change your emotional state

Our emotional state affects our body quite significantly as I'm sure you already know. What you may not know is that our body affects our emotional state to an equal degree.

A study was done at the University of Illinois in 1984. In the study, one group of students were told to grip a pencil using their lips and asked to write by holding the pencil in this way. After this, the researchers then asked the students to watch a cartoon with the pencil still in their mouth. The second group of students were asked to do the same as this, only this time they had to hold the pencil with their teeth. The students were then asked to rate the cartoon afterwards.

The test was on "facial feedback hypothesis". The theory was that we don't just smile because we are happy, but we can become happy because we smile, and that it works both ways. What they found was that the students who held the pencil with their teeth; enjoyed the cartoon significantly more than the other group. These students were unconsciously emulating a smile resulting in an increased enjoyment of the cartoon. The students who held the pencil with their lips emulated a frown resulting in them being more likely to dislike the cartoon.

The hypothesis was proved correct and many studies since then have backed up this theory.

Embodying a feeling

This knowledge shows us that we can very easily change our emotions using our body. Not only do we stand confidently when we are in a confident state, but we can feel confident by merely standing that way.

When we are worried, it is often good to take on the feeling of confidence. This is because we become much more competent decision makers when we feel we can handle a situation. We can use our brains full potential rather than limit our thoughts by worrying.

Embodying a feeling is when you take on a feeling that you are currently not experiencing. You copy the sensations in your body of how it would feel to be in that state.

For example, if you want to feel smart, remember a time when you felt smart. Then mirror how you felt and take on the body language you had. Focus on how it would feel and try to embody it.

If you want to feel relaxed, focus on a time when you were relaxed and ask yourself how it would feel? Then once again, embody it and match your body language to this feeling.

After this, you can think of a word or a phrase that encapsulates the feeling. You can then start to move like you would in this emotional state. How would you walk differently, how would your body feel and how would you express yourself in this desired state? Combine all of these aspects to develop the ability to change your emotional state at will.

A thing to note here is how you are asking the questions of how it would feel instead of telling yourself you are indeed feeling that way. I will explain this subtle nuance later in the book.

Priming your emotional state

If you want to prime your emotional state you can also utilize your body using the following warm up exercise.

- Start by stretching out your arms as wide as you can, with your palms facing up.

- Roll your head back towards the sky and create a big over-exaggerated smile or laugh.

This works by exaggerating the positioning of your body when you feel happy and confident. If you do this for 20 seconds, you should feel very good and improving the way you feel enhances your ability to act. This is a combination of a few methods. Athletes will often perform activities like this in a mental warm up before an event.

Our bodies can be used to easily and rapidly change our emotional state and it is a very useful tool to have in our arsenal to pull out when needed.

Asking yourself questions that alter your emotional state

One effective way to change your emotional state is to ask cleverly crafted questions that benefit you. We can access the creative part of our mind when we do this. This will start to change the emotional part of our brains. By asking ourselves questions, the mind engages to start looking for solutions. This process is automatic. When it does start to search for an answer; you have already changed your thought patterns. If you ask questions that force you to see the positives of a situation you will begin to switch from negatively associating with the event, to positively associating with it. This then will cause our emotions to follow suit.

For example, if you are running a business and something doesn't go too well. Ask yourself "How could this be a benefit to me and my business later on?" or "In what way could I improve my product so this wouldn't happen?"

If you are in a worrisome depressed state, ask yourself the question, "What am I grateful for in my life right now?"

Questions like "In what way could this benefit me?" and others of that nature will help to quickly change your emotional state.

At first, your mind will resist and tell you there is no answer. You must keep asking the questions and the answers will begin to arise. This is the power of asking questions compared to telling yourself statements. If you were to keep telling yourself when you are in a state of worry, for example, "This is going to benefit me!" You will be met with strong resistance. Your mind won't simply allow you to alter your emotions by trying to force thoughts upon it. If anything this will help reinforce your current emotional state. It would be acting as a source of denial and as we spoke about before, acceptance is key.

By asking questions; answers arise much more organically for the brain, and it is easier for it to accept. When it starts to come up with these positive answers to your questions, your emotional state will begin to change.

So always remember to come up with ingenious questions that you can ask yourself that will change your emotional state, and keep asking them until your mind starts creating answers.

Changing sub-modalities of fears and memories

As we have talked about before when things don't go our way; it can often set us into a spiral of negative thought loops. We keep remembering and reliving an event keeping us in that current emotional state. Changing the sub-modalities of these memories helps us to scramble the memory and disassociate the negative emotion from it.

The process:

- Take your memory and watch it in your mind as if it were a movie. Just try to watch it and observe it. Don't get upset about it; you are merely watching it as it happened.

- Take the experience and turn it into a cartoon. Smile as you watch it and then begin to run it backward. Watching everything going backward and people swallowing their words as you move back through the movie. Let the movie run back in very fast motion. Now run it forward in an even faster motion. This time, change colors in the movie so that the people's faces in the movie are multicolored and psychedelic.

- If there's a particular person in the movie that has bothered you, start changing some of their features. Make their ears and nose humorously big. Whatever you can think of that you find particularly funny.

- Do this process at least ten times fast forwarding and rewinding as you please and increasing the humor and sub-modalities of the movie. Maybe even add in some cartoon music or a funny song.

- The important aspects of this method are the speed in which you play/rewind it and the humor you add to it. After you followed this process, think back to your memory and notice if you still feel the same way about it. If you have done it correctly or long enough you should have broken the emotional pattern you associate with it.

You can also perform this with future fears when imagining what might go wrong and then change its sub-modalities.

This is a very useful and playful method that can come in very handy to quickly get over something and change your emotional state.

Free from outcome and the art of putting

We can be sling-shotted into a state of mental panic when we are fixated on an outcome and then realize that it may be stripped away from us. When this mental panic hits, we distance ourselves even further from that desired result. Our body and mind begin working against us.

The reason well prepared students go blank in an exam is because they need the outcome too badly. They need it so badly in fact, that their mind becomes filled with worry. This significantly limits its capacity to think properly at that moment. Their desire for their goal has transformed from a motivator to an inhibitor of their success.

As I mentioned before, I was a victim of this during exams in school. One of the skills I learned to overcome this has since then proved very useful. I believe the first time I read about this technique was in reference to sports psychology. It was talking about how desire gives an athlete an immediate advantage. They will work harder than someone with less desire. It then followed up showing that the ironic thing about desire was that it then actually damaged their performance if they cared too much. It limited their ability to truly express themselves in their sport as they became overtaken by the fear of not performing.

So a balance must be found between wanting something too much and wanting it too little. The following technique can be useful to do this. To explain the technique, I'm going to compare it to putting in golf. When a golfer is on the green and preparing to put the ball into the hole. He must hold two things in his mind when deciding on how to hit the shot. He must believe that when he hits the ball that it is going to go in the hole. However, he must also keep in mind that he must hit the ball in a way that if he misses; it doesn't end up too far away from the hole. Now you may notice that these two thoughts are essentially paradoxical. One thought cannot exist if the other does. You would be right about this, but the human brain does have the capacity to hold two contrasting beliefs at the same time. It is in this way the following process works.

If you find worry taking over you and hindering your ability to think. Start to convince yourself that it doesn't in fact matter. You are to hold it on a conscious level that you do not care about the outcome. You are to convince yourself that the event itself is more of a practice session for events to come later. You can view the event as a way to develop your work ethic rather than your results. Tell yourself that you will need your work ethic for a much more important future occasion. The outcome in this situation is completely irrelevant; all that matters is the work you put in and the preparation you have taken for greater things to come.

For example, if you have an important presentation that you feel that you must get right. In the beginning, your desire has created an advantage of emotional leverage. This will help you to put in the ground work. However, when it comes down to the speech itself, the need for it to work will start to work against you. To counteract this, once you have put the work in and you know everything inside out; it's time to alter your thoughts.

Now you will start convincing yourself on a conscious level that this presentation is completely irrelevant. It's just an occasion to home your skills for big presentations ten years from now. Its outcome is completely irrelevant as you are heading for much more significant opportunities. It is merely a practice session.

Make sure to continue to actively reinforce this belief by brushing off the event's importance.

Of course, deep down you know it matters to you as you would not have put the work in otherwise. This is essentially brainwashing yourself in order to help you achieve what you are capable of.

Once again if we were trying to force beliefs upon us that the presentation was going to go well, our mind could meet us with resistance against this. All we are doing is taking the importance out of the outcome.

This is meant as a type of preparation after you have put in the work. Notice this is only an idea to balance your emotional state if you are too dependent on an outcome. If that is not the case, it will only work against your ability to do the work necessary.

Developing self-discipline

Our ability to delay instant gratification for a more long term reward is extremely useful when achieving our goals. With our lizard brain continuously getting us to procrastinate and take the easy option it can be hard to stick to our commitments. The following examples are some fairly simple methods and principles you can follow to start to gain some momentum in achieving your goals.

Before you start any new discipline or path to a goal, you need to know one thing very well before you begin.

You must start with your reason for "Why" you are doing what you are doing. It can't be vague or just a surface level knowledge of this. You must have a very deep understanding of why you are doing what you are doing and have an extensive knowledge of all the benefits you will receive through completing your goal.

The next step is to start small and set a little goal that is easily achievable. This will baby step the process of starting any new task. By starting small, you have created something in your mind that you believe you can achieve. You have lowered the pain that you have to go through in order to achieve your first goal. Then once you have achieved this goal, you can introduce a second slightly larger goal. By continuing with this process, you are taking baby steps that get the ball rolling to your new activity and this can give you the momentum of achieving.

The next stage of what you want to do is to change your process into a habit that you perform without much thought. When you do this, your activity requires less mental energy, and will thus be easier to complete. The process has become instinctual and you do not need to use up will-power to do it anymore. Long term this is the most sustainable way of maintaining disciplines.

One other useful trick that often is not utilized is using visualization to aid the process. Visualizing your success may seem counterproductive, as you may think it is wasting time you could spend working. However, visualization does one very important thing. Our subconscious mind can be very easily influenced by what we visualize. It struggles to tell the difference between what we think in our minds and the outside reality. So when you are consciously reinforcing the vision of you achieving what you want, your mind will start to believe your goal is a lot more attainable. This then helps to keep you motivated with the belief that you will do what you set out to do.

These are merely a few concepts to help you begin to tame your lizard brain. The more you do tame it, the better you get at doing so.

Living by principles, having integrity and eliminating unnecessary worry and distress

So many events in the universe are outside of our control. A person with a high EQ only focuses on what they can influence rather than worrying about what they can't. Something we can never control is the outcome of our actions. So many of us are emotionally guided by our outcomes. We derive our sense of self from them. Due to this, we are always at mercy to the vast unpredictability of the universe.

To deal with this we can change what we place our focus on. Thus changing what we derive our sense of selves from. By living a life guided by principles and integrity instead of external results we take back this control that we have passed off.

Often we can get caught up by the results of our actions. If they end up badly due to unforeseen circumstances it causes us mental distress. For example, if your actions led to something that caused discomfort for those around you or yourself. You might then feel a sense of guilt. By living by principles, you learn to understand the only thing you can control is if you had good intentions or not. Everything else is out of your control. We can only ever do the best we can with the knowledge we currently have. We as humans do not yet possess the gift of foresight and as long as we set out with good intentions, then we shouldn't take it too much to heart. All you can do is apply the knowledge you have gained to better prepare yourself for future decisions. It is not the best option to extract the knowledge of whether we are a good or bad person from external results. Instead, we should extract this from the only thing we have control over and that is our intentions behind our actions. Results are merely feedback to be used to improve our future decisions.

To live a life of principles, it is important to know firstly what your principles are before you are put on the spot to make a decision. It's a very beneficial exercise to write out your principles and what you stand for. A principle is something you can control such as your work ethic.

So take some time out to think of and write out your principles now and this way you'll know immediately how to act once the time comes.

To help you along with the process here are some of my basic principles that I live my life by. I have written these out in a lot greater detail than this and significantly elaborated upon them, but they will give you a gist of some things you could write.

- I always have good intentions but I am willing to stand up for myself if I need to.

- I chase after what I want in life and I'm willing to fail.

- I work hard for what I want in life and I'm willing to make sacrifices for it.

The next step once you know what your principles are, is to live by them with absolute integrity and do not break them. Continuously evaluate and update them, but stick with them and have impeccable integrity.

Following these guidelines will help you focus on what you can control in your life rather than worrying and feeling guilty about what you no control over.

Taking responsibility

Another mindset I would encourage you to have is that of accepting full responsibility for everything that has you as a contributing factor in it. At first, this may seem strange or even damaging to your emotional mind, but there is a major benefit to doing this. When we accept responsibility for it, that means we essentially have the ability to change it. We then stop reacting to what is happening to us and start acting and creating the changes ourselves.

Even if you are only 1% of the input and 99% was from elsewhere; accept responsibility for it and start looking at ways you could have safeguarded or changed the process to change the odds. This starts to change your mind from a victim mentality to a more productive approach. It shifts you from complaining and resenting the other contributors to focusing on what was in your control.

For example, if you are a boss in a company, and you designate a project. It's time to launch and you look at the product only to find that it is nowhere near up to scratch. It's too late to change. You could spend time complaining about how useless your employees are but this would ultimately not solve anything. However, if you use this new found approach, you would look at what could you have done differently and what you could do to prevent this from happening in future. It could be as simple as checking up on your employee's work every so often. You could then see if they are heading in the right direction. If you haven't got time for this, employ someone to do it for you or designate the task to a current employee. The first mindset is a waste of time and energy. The second mindset will help you to improve for future projects and help you to prevent repeat occurrences.

When you start addressing this, you will not only become more productive, but you will also be more in control of your emotional state.

James L. Austin

Learning How To Read People And Grasping Social Awareness

Social awareness is so important to our everyday lives. It allows us to see the points of view of the people around us. When we develop this aspect of EQ, we learn to pick up subtle cues and expressions that give us insight to the people we interact with. These cues act as a feedback to tell us how they feel, and what their intentions may be. This is the basis of empathy.

A game of behavioral awareness

Poker players are world experts at reading people as their job line depends on it. I remember watching a poker tournament on television a few years back. There were only two men left in the game and it was the final in which they were playing for a cash sum of one million dollars.

One guy looks very much as if he is in a motorcycle gang with his long beard and studded denim jacket. The other is a young kid who couldn't be more than twenty and is wearing a hoody with his hood up. The kid is doing this because he isn't a natural to the poker table, at least not in the physical sense. He comes from the online world of poker and this was where he learned the trade. Because of this, however, he doesn't have as high of a social intuition and ability to read others as the other man, well at least not yet. He also is not as aware of what signals he is giving off to the other players. So he has his hood up to mask his face as much as possible. A common thing to do among internet poker stars.

The bearded man has a full house in his hand and is fairly certain on his impending victory as this is a very strong hand. The kid, however, has four of a kind which outranks the bearded man. The kid decides to go all in as you would expect with such a strong hand.

The bearded man stares at him intently, trying to spot a chink in his armor and trying to understand what is going on in his head. The kid leans forward, putting his elbows on the table and linking his fingers together blocking his face. He is in an almost prayer like position; only his top two fingers are pointed out straight, and meeting each other like a chess player. You can see the bearded man starting to perspire; he believes he could wipe this kid out now with one blow, and win the money. Just to be sure he employs patience to work as his ally.

The bearded man talks to the kid, but the kid doesn't say anything back. The kid is still sitting in the same position with his hood up. The bearded man gets up off his chair, starts to pace around the room and pondering the possible scenarios. He then stops and turns around and sits at the table once more. He stares intently at the kid focusing extremely hard to try to understand what is going on inside the young man's head. The bearded man now begins to mirror the kid's body language on his seat and emulate him exactly. He is trying to get a sense of what the kid is feeling. The bearded man looks up and says "I'm out."

The bearded man has just lost over half his pot to the kid and has no idea if he had made the right call as he never seen the kid's cards. The bearded man then goes on and wins the game regardless. An interviewer after it described the scenario and told him the hand the kid had at that stage of the game. If he hadn't of made that decision, he would have lost the game. The interviewer asked with amazement "How did you know?" The man replied, "I just copied his body language, I sat how he sat and tried to understand how I would feel to sit in that way, I felt pretty confident, so luckily I folded." The man's social intuition was a finely tuned instrument that allowed him to win the game.

Poker players are a prime example of how we can develop our intuition through developing reference experiences for our mind. These are not abilities that they were naturally born with but a skill they have carefully trained through practice. Our social intuition can be significantly advanced with focused effort.

Watch, interpret and predict

A good way to boost your ability to read people is to first understand yourself. What do you do when you feel uncomfortable, angry and so on? Start to notice and become aware of this. Once you do so, you can then take it to the next level. You can start people watching, and trying to interpret what their situation is. You can then try to predict what is going to happen next. If you start to do this, you will notice patterns as they arise, and it will develop your intuition.

It is said that only ten percent of conversation is the words we say. Everything else is communicated through our sub-communications. Sub-communications are subtle cues and micro-expressions that we all give off. They help others to subconsciously judge how we are feeling.

When someone is uncomfortable they usually do some of the following:

- They break eye contact.
- Their shoulders tense up.
- They might give a nervous laugh.

These might be because of something you have said or they could simply be nervous. If you want to alleviate the pressure they feel allowing them to feel more comfortable; try taking a slight step back and changing the topic. Moving your body back even slightly will alleviate the pressure. Another way to alleviate this pressure is through smiling. This helps you sub-communicate to them that you are happy they are there.

Confidence is usually signified by the following traits:

- Good tall posture.
- Chin up.
- Shoulders rolled back with their chest out.
- When confident people make gestures, they often take up more space with their hands because they are more comfortable in the environment.
- They will also usually have very good strong eye contact.

People with low self-confidence are usually the opposite: Their shoulders will be rolled forward, their head will often be down, they will have unsteady eye contact, and they are often weary of taking up too much space.

Becoming present to the moment

This is another area in which meditation can help us to vastly improve in. It helps reduce the effect that our self-image has on our perception of the world. Because of this meditation allows you to see and acknowledge different points of view. It also helps to increase your awareness of what is going on around you. It does this because it helps to train us to become present to the moment. What this means is that we are not focused on the past, the future or the thoughts going on in our head. Instead, we are solely focused on this moment. Since the mind is solely focused on this moment, the brain can work much better, and more efficiently than before. Our attention is not as scattered. People who are witty for example tend to be people who are extremely present during conversation. This then allows them to be faster off the mark to a joke. They are listening and paying attention to what is going on and what is being said.

A master of charisma, in general, was ex-president of the United States of America, Bill Clinton. It was said that one of his most recognizable traits was his ability to make everyone he talked to feel special. He had a skill of conveying to people that he was listening, and feeling what they were feeling. This was because he was. When you develop presence, you refine your skill of listening and reading people.

With your full focus on this moment, you access your full brain power to read, interpret, and feel what other people are feeling. This translates to others extremely well. They can sense when someone is listening to them.

Noticing cultural differences

What may be seen as polite, and inviting in some cultures, can be considered rude in others. It is important to begin to interpret the cultural differences between different countries and even different social occasions. In a western culture, for example, strong eye contact is a sign of confidence and trustworthiness, whereas in some parts of Asia it can be seen as extremely rude. In Japan slurping your soup is considered polite whereas in western culture it is frowned upon. There are so many cultural differences that it is important to notice them, and learn them when the occasion arises.

What do you mean?

Words are just the surface of communication. People can say something and mean something entirely different. By learning to stay present and start to observe subtle differences, and cues you can begin to see the deeper meaning behind the words. You can learn to pick up on the micro expressions on other people's faces. These will give you an indication of their intent or how they are feeling. This is a much deeper level of communication that is often overlooked yet it is vital.

Our social intuition can be trained with focused effort. If you want to develop this intuition, place your awareness on how what you are saying is making other people around you feel. Try to notice the subtle nuances in their facial expressions. Can you notice if a person is laughing, but holding a bit of facial tension because what you have said has hurt them? Can you notice if something you have said has made people uncomfortable and yet they are trying to hide it? Noticing these differences and developing your awareness is such an important skill for life.

Relationship Management

Having the right connections gets deals, promotions and opens doors up for us. Our ability to manage our relationships is crucial for not only a successful life but for a happy one.

Destroying pedestals and objectification for second to none results

When dealing with people of authority and status, there is one major flawed mindset we take on. We view them as being above us and we thus objectify them to an extent. This is often the reason why we run out of things to say when we talk to those we view as high status. It is not due to our lack of ability to talk. I'm sure you will agree that when you're with your friends or family, you can talk forever. The reason you are short for words is because you are placing such a high criteria on the words that come out of your mouth. This then significantly limits what you deem as acceptable to say out loud. If this happens to a high enough extent, you will not be able to think of anything at all to say.

The trick here is to quite simply begin to view them as human beings. They have worries and fears just the same as everyone else does. When you stop building them up like this, it becomes a lot easier to develop a relationship with them. You can begin to talk to them like a normal person. This then allows them to be able to create a much stronger connection with you. As easy as it is to get carried away with their status do not let yourself fall victim to it. If you do, you will severely reduce your chances of forming a meaningful bond with them.

I developed this knowledge quite a while ago now when I was learning how to get a mentor for business. The idea's pretty basic, people of high value are surrounded by people who are constantly being fake to them. To stand out and create any relationship with them you can start by being down to earth and treating them as you would do to anyone else.

Knowing this, you can begin to monitor your behavior around those of perceived high status and then begin to systematically destroy the pedestals that you have placed them on.

The ultimate ingredients to any successful relationship

Relationships are often a means of value exchange just like any financial transaction. They ideally should be formed with a win/win for those involved. It is an unsustainable method to create relationships on a win/lose basis. This is how people of low EQ will conduct their relationships. It is essentially taking more than you are giving, and leaves one side slightly jaded. If you ask a lot of your friends, you must be prepared to give a lot back. It is a value exchange and value can be anything in nature that benefits them. Something as simple as being there for them when they need you or being able to cheer them up by making them laugh. These are all things that add value to a relationship. If you view it like a bank account, you must put money in to the account so that later you can take money out. If you are constantly taking money out of the account and not putting any in the relationship will become strained.

When forming a new relationship, it is important to start putting money into this metaphorical bank account by adding value. If you begin by asking for too much off the bat; you will drive relationships away and stop any bond from forming. Everything from business to loving relationships all follow this principle. I don't recommend viewing it as you are giving to receive, but rather to remind you to give back to those who give value to your life. Ideally, you will want to give without expectation which I will talk about later in the book.

The longer you have money in a bank account, the more interest your money will receive. Similar to this, the longer you have a relationship with someone, the more you can ask of them. You can ask for bigger favors from childhood friends, for example, than you could do to someone you have just met. You will have a stronger connection with someone the longer you know them and the more interactions you have as you have built a level of trust and nostalgia between both of you.

Constantly complaining to your friends is the equivalent of continuously taking money out. They will begin to develop negative associations with you. The same goes for if you are constantly asking for their time, and giving nothing in return. Negative associations will then lead to one of two results. Either the relationship will end, or resentment will build. If resentment does build it will find other ways to be satisfied such as passive aggressive actions.

Try to become aware of any relationships where you take more than you give and try to think of ways you could change this balance. It could be as simple as being in a happy mood around them.

Conflict Resolution 101

There are essentially five ways of dealing with confrontation: Denial/avoiding it, smoothing over the problem, compromise/negotiation, competing/fighting and collaboration.

Denial or avoiding problems isn't a healthy way of dealing with them. It leads to emotions like resentment and only allows a problem to build up. It is very psychologically damaging to be using this as your method on a regular basis.

Smoothing over the problem also doesn't solve the problem; it merely masks its effects on the surface.

Compromise and negotiation is an improvement as both sides will receive smaller than full victories. A lot of the time this may not be achievable.

As regards to fighting or competition, this is a very poor method of dealing with issues. In this method, both people waste time and energy, and it is a win/lose scenario. If you are constantly carrying out your life using this method, it will be emotionally draining.

The best way if you can achieve it, is collaboration; this is a win/win for both parties. When you are constantly creating win/win deals, the chance of someone accepting those deals is much higher. To reach a stage of collaboration, we must first understand the other person's point of view. Seek to understand, before you seek a solution. As both people thinking of solutions that benefit themselves the most will limit the potential ideas. However, if your main goal from the start is to seek to understand the other person and then to engineer a solution, you will have a far broader way of looking at things.

There was a mathematics riddle I read once about a father who had died. He split his inheritance up between his three sons. The inheritance consisted of 17 camels. He said in his will for his eldest son to have 1/2 of the camels, the middle son to have 1/3 rd of the camels, and the youngest son to have 1/9 of them. However, the sons had a problem with this. 17 does not divide by 9, nor 3 or 2 without a remainder. They started to fight over the number of camels each of them will receive.

Eventually, they decide to go to a wise old man in the village. They explain the problem to the wise man. He takes a second of thought and says "I will give you my camel; then you will have 18 camels. You can divide 18 by 2, 3 and 9 without a remainder." So the eldest son took 9 of the camels, the middle son took 6 of them and the youngest took two of them. The sons then say, "Now there's one camel extra." The wise man says, "I will take that one back."

The goal in any conflict is to find a middle ground like the wise man's camel in the story and from there you can create something that benefits all parties.

Verbal Judo To Deal With Confrontation

This is the art of choosing to meet confrontation not with confrontation, but essentially using other people's attack and turning it into something else, similar to the martial art Judo. In George J Thompson's book "Verbal Judo", he goes into grave detail on this method. He was a retired police officer who has an extremely impressive background in dealing with confrontation in the most intense situations.

One of his main responses to dealing with a confrontation is not what you'd expect. In fact, he usually starts off by agreeing with the attacker's statement and using it in what he calls a deflector move. He immediately says one of these deflector statements such as: "I appreciate that you feel that way but..." or "I understand that, but..." This is a rapport making a statement with a person who you otherwise you wouldn't have been able to develop a connection with.

For example, if someone started a verbal insult calling you "Fat." In this method, you would say something along the lines of "I appreciate where you're coming from; I could do with losing a few pounds. I think my wife would agree with you." Immediately you have disarmed the entire insult as well as dealing with it.

Once people know they can't get to you they will usually stop.

In one of Georges stories he talks about how his son had come home with a report card where he had gotten 4 A's, and an F. George immediately wanted to bring up the F in an angry manner, however, he chose a smarter route.

He said to his son, "Wow, four A's, I've never got that in my life, well done," and then walked off. His son asked, "Aren't you going to ask about the F?" George replied, "No, if you're smart enough to get 4 A's, I realized that you must have done this on purpose." The son says "Yea I did, aren't you going to ask why?" George replied, "Alright then why?" His son then explains how he didn't like his teacher. George says "Well that ought to show him," in a sarcastic tone. The son curious to know what he meant by this asked, "Why?" George explains, "If I had a teacher like that, I'd want to make him give me a good grade, that would be harder for him to do." His son thought about this before walking off.

Six weeks later, his son handed him a report card showing how he had pulled his grade up to a B. If George had of reacted badly to his son's grades he would have just been met with resistance from his son. However, he chose to delay his immediate emotional reaction and chose a path which led to the best outcome for him and his son.

Our immediate emotional reaction is often not the most beneficial one. We can choose to deal with problems in a much more logical and goal-orientated way. This allows us to achieve the best solution.

Knowing the meaning behind our words

As we have talked about in the previous sections, our words are just the surface level of our communication. So it is important to know, and understand our intent behind our words. By knowing and understanding our intent we communicate assertiveness and that we can be trusted. This is communicated through us constantly giving off sub-communications that act as honest signals. These tell people if we are authentic or not. When we say one thing, but have a completely different intention it will come off as inauthentic. I think we can all recall a person who comes off as fake to us. Even when we have no conscious evidence of why we feel this way. This is due to them having a different intent than what the portray through their words.

I remember working in a bar when I was younger, one of the bosses had a very poor way of communicating. He would always make up excuses for the work he set you. For example, he would say something along the lines of "Can you clean the top of them fridges, my lungs are bad and I can't do it." The problem here wasn't because he was asking people to do this work. This can be expected as he was our boss. It was the fact that he would always make up an excuse for you to do it. He wasn't being authentic. His intent was divided between asking us to do the work and trying to make us like him. This then affected his word choice, and how he conveyed his message. This was a sign of poor relationship management and would have the opposite to the desired effect. It would have been very different if he had stated it in a way such as "Can you clean the top of those fridges for me?" If we dissect the meaning behind these words, it would be that he needs the employee to clean the fridges for him, but he still treats the employee with the respect to ask him. The resultant action is the same but the second way would be much more authentic. The intent of these words is clear and thus much more effective.

In the same way honest signals work against you if you do not have a clear intent, they will work against you if you are pretending to be someone you are not.

It's a common occurrence for people with a low EQ to try to take on an identity that they think the other person will accept. An example of this would be the person who pretends they like sports when they do not. It is essentially dishonest. It sends off these honest signals that tell the other person there is something off with you. You may lose a talking point through being honest, but it is the foundation for a much stronger bond. Also as a byproduct, you will be treated with more respect.

So to be authentic, say what you mean in a way in which it is congruent to your intention or goal and don't pretend to be something you're not.

How to criticize others effectively

There was a study on applied psychology in regards to the effect of destructive criticism on conflict, self-efficacy, and task performance. Two groups of people were observed during the study.

In group number one, 83 undergraduates either received constructive or destructive criticism of their work. Those who were dealt with by using deconstructive criticism reported greater anger, and tension levels. They also indicated that in future they would be less likely to opt for more collaborative or negotiation methods in dealing with conflict.

In the second study, 106 graduates who received destructive criticism of their initial work, then proceeded to set lower goals. They also had lower self-efficacy on two additional tasks compared to the people who received no feedback or constructive criticism.

Often when people criticize others ineffectively, the resultant change is in the opposite direction than desired. An employee who feels overly criticized will lose passion for their work and their mental attitude will change to one of doing the bare minimum. To effectively criticize someone, you must have a foundation of praise. This praise cannot be for nothing, but instead from when they have done things well. This then gives you a much better place to criticize them from.

It is also important to realize that you should criticize the action, rather than the person. There is a significant psychological difference between the two. If you criticize someone, for example calling them "stupid" it can damage their self-esteem. By doing so, it will cause them to attach very strong negative emotions to their work. The resultant change will most likely be a decrease of their passion for their job. However, if you criticize their actions, for example, "That was a stupid mistake, come on, I need you to be better than this." The employee learns that they have messed up. They gain the understanding not to do it again. However, they will learn in a much more beneficial way for the both of you.

We need not shy away from criticism, but there should always be a goal to it. We can create a win/win scenario once again if we are smart and logical about what we decide to say.

The difference between nice and kind

These two adjectives are often used interchangeably, but there is a stark contrast in the meaning behind them. To be "nice" is to be agreeable, and to avoid conflict or friction at all costs to appear pleasant from the outside to society. Kindness is to have compassion from within and behave accordingly even if it doesn't appear pleasant to the outside world. The difference is subtle, but hugely important. From a young age, we are constantly taught to be kind, to get on well with everyone we meet, and to cause minimal hassle. However, this can be extremely damaging to our psychology and our relationships.

There is one big killer to all relationships, and that is resentment. By following the nice method of dealing with things we often suppress our emotions. We don't learn to deal with them in a healthy way. For example, if someone interacts with you in a way in which you don't like. The nice method is to keep quiet and not say anything. However, as this behavior continues your resentment will begin to grow towards them. If the resentment is not dealt with, it will find a way to be released.

One way in which resentment is relieved is through passive aggressive actions or comments. This is an attempt to get back at the person in a more indirect way. The person is unable to straight up tell them the problem; so this is the result. It can be damaging and hurtful to the other person and destroys relationships.

Resentment can also lead to a buildup of emotion until eventually there is an outburst. There are lots of cases in a work environment in which an employee who has no history of acting out does so. Despite this never happening before, they lash out in the office after something trivial. This was not caused by one event in itself, but instead a buildup of emotions. This happens because their resentment was never dealt with. It got to such an unhealthy extent that the emotion needed to be released and the person completely lost control. In a lot of these cases, the people who lash out are considered by everyone around them as nice people. They have just suppressed their emotions so long that they need to be released in some form. Their nice mentality has led to this unhealthy lifestyle.

Giving more than you have to give

Often when we are overly nice, we behave in an unbalanced way. We give more than we can and don't make sure to take care of ourselves. This sounds noble, but it has serious consequences on our relationships. When you give before you have taken care of your own needs, you have placed the other person's needs before your own. When your needs aren't covered, you then begin to develop resentment towards the person you believe caused this. Once again resentment leaks into the relationship and it will need to be resolved.

I remember before I had learned this aspect of emotional intelligence I had a very important exam in college that I was in no way prepared for. It was only a few days after another exam and I had very little time to prepare for it. Every second of studying counted at this stage and I was a day away from it. I was in the middle of studying when my friend Alex phoned me up. He had not done enough preparation for his coursework. He had anticipated that another friend would be able to help him out. This friend became unavailable to help him. He did not have enough time to study the parts of the course that he didn't know. So he would not be able to complete it on time. Alex knew I was good at mathematics; he needed my help. He begged and pleaded with me and I reluctantly agreed. The coursework only took about two hours to complete, but it was two hours that I didn't have to give.

Later he found out he passed his coursework with flying colors, and I found out that I had failed my exam by 1%. This was an end of year exam which went towards my degree. I had failed it. This meant I had to do a repeat exam during summer and my mark was capped at 40%. I was furious at him for costing me that time when I needed it. I complained about it multiple times, I didn't talk to him for a few weeks, and when I did it was tangled with resentment.

Whenever I look back to this now, I don't see Alex as the one who is at fault. It was very clearly me. It was my decisions that caused this result and so I am to blame. I should have told Alex the truth from the start and concentrated on my work. It was Alex's responsibility to make sure that he was covered for his work and not mine. If I had said no, he would probably have been able to find someone else who could have helped him or suffered the consequences of his mistake. By putting Alex first, I wasn't making our friendship stronger, but instead doing something that threatened it. I did something that caused me to resent my friend which was extremely damaging to our friendship. We are still good friends thankfully, but I still keep in mind the lesson I learned from this.

Putting yourself in the other person's shoes. Would you rather your friends and loved ones put you first in their lives and resented, even hated you for it behind your back or would you rather they be upfront and honest with you? The answer is obviously the second one.

The situation would have been different if I did not have that exam and I instead had to put off something less important. It would also have been different if Alex needed me for something more important than an exam. We must learn to clearly assess the situation in order to figure out if putting someone else first is the right action.

So although we may believe our actions of putting other's needs before our own are good for our relationships, they may be the very thing that will destroy them. You must learn to recognize that your own needs are important and from this much more emotionally grounded place, then decide what the right thing for the both of you is to do. Sometimes, putting others needs before our own isn't the kind thing to do, instead, the kind thing to do is to be upfront with those around us.

Our internal contracts

Often when we behave in a nice manner, we also create internal contracts in our heads. We can do nice things for people that we believe are with no strings attached. Yet we are unaware that we have created a certain expectation of the other person in our heads.

I remember a friend of mine called Paul told me a few years ago he wanted to start going to the gym and getting in shape. I then proceeded to tell him I would draw him up a gym plan to help him out with this. So I drew one up for him on the computer and worked out what type of program he would benefit the most from. I put a lot of thought and effort into it and then printed it out and gave it to him.

I followed up with him a couple of weeks later about it. To my disappointment, he had not been going as the program had stated to go. He would thus not get the results he wanted. I was extremely annoyed at this as I had gone to all this effort to help him out and he had just neglected it.

After a while, I realized that my actions weren't out of kindness after all, but simply from me being nice. I had created a mental contract in my head that my friend Paul had no idea about. The contract went something similar to "I will spend time and effort to draw up this plan, but if I do; you have to follow it exactly for the duration of the program." It was not Paul's fault for the misunderstanding; it was mine.

I should have outwardly stated that if I were to spend the time to draw one up for him that I expected him to follow it. If I had done this, then it is a fair agreement to which he could say yes or no. If he were to say yes, and if didn't keep to his word; then I would have had a right to be annoyed at him. I would learn for the next time not to do something like this for him again. In this situation, he would also have known that he had broken the agreement which is much more fair.

Often the other person can be completely oblivious to this imaginary contract. Then when they do break this contract, it creates a feeling of resentment from us towards them. When we are truly kind there is no contract; we give without expectation. It is unfair to hold someone accountable for something they didn't even know existed.

When I first studied this concept, I found out that I was very guilty of doing this. I immediately saw all the scenarios in my life where I unfairly judged someone for breaking conditions that they didn't even know existed. Try to think about situations in your own life to which this concept applies and start to see where you may have passed an unfair judgment.

Kindness is never followed by resentment of any sort. If you are feeling resentment towards someone in your life it is important you learn to deal with it and the best way is to be upfront and honest.

Conclusion

So you now know EQ is something you can very easily develop for it to have very significant effects on your life. I hope you learned such things as the importance of EQ, the different aspects of it, how to become more aware of yourself and others, and how to manage your emotions and your relationships in a more effective way.

This is such crucial area of success which often is not utilized, but in which you now know about. However, knowledge alone is not enough. The next step is to use your new found knowledge, and implement it in all areas of your life to help you to achieve the success that you always wanted.

Thank you.

Notes

What Is Emotional Intelligence and Why Is It So Important For Success

Lizard brain

Godin, S., Hagy, J. and MacLeod, H. (2011) *Linchpin: Are you indispensable?* New York: Penguin Group (USA).

Pressfield, S. (2012) *The War of Art: Break through the blocks and win your inner creative battles*. New York: Black Irish Entertainment.

Affect, generalization, and the perception of risk.
Johnson, Eric J.; Tversky, Amos
Journal of Personality and Social Psychology, Vol 45(1), Jul 1983, 20-31.http://dx.doi.org/10.1037/0022-3514.45.1.20

Lincoln, R. and Photographer, H.S. (2012) *Decoding keys to a healthy life*. Available at: http://news.harvard.edu/gazette/story/2012/02/decoding-keys-to-a-healthy-life/ (Accessed: 20 August 2016).

Studies on Mirror Neurons

Comment and Murdock, G. (2013) *Reflections on mirror Neurons - association for psychological science*. Available at: http://www.psychologicalscience.org/index.php/publications/observer/2011/march-11/reflections-on-mirror-neurons.html (Accessed: 20 August 2016).

TEDx Talks (2010) *TEDxGöteborg - Gustaf Gredebäck - the mirror neuron system: Understanding others as oneself.* Available at: https://www.youtube.com/watch?v=DY1HAJGpyVw (Accessed: 20 August 2016).

Studies on the link between emotional intelligence and annual salary.

Bradberry, T., Greaves, J. and Lencioni, P. (2005) *The emotional intelligence quick book: Everything you need to know to put your EQ to work.* New York: Simon & Schuster Adult Publishing Group.

James L. Austin

The Four Areas of Emotional Intelligence And Why They Matter

The Four Skills of Emotional Intelligence and Emotional hijacking

Goleman, D., Boyatzis, R., McKee, A. and Goleman, P.D. (2013) *Primal Leadership: Unleashing the power of emotional intelligence, with a new preface by.* 10th edn. Boston, MA, United States: Harvard Business Review Press.

Competencies of relationship management

dgadmin (2015) *Daniel Goleman: How emotionally intelligent are you?* Available at: http://www.danielgoleman.info/daniel-goleman-how-emotionally-intelligent-are-you/ (Accessed: 20 August 2016).

Developing Emotional Awareness

Research on Emotionally priming teachers

Yale University (2013) *Emotional Intelligence: From theory to everyday practice*. Available at: https://www.youtube.com/watch?v=e8JMWtwdLQ4 (Accessed: 20 August 2016).

Emotional State

Robbins and Robbins, A. (1992) *Awaken the giant within How to take immediate control of your mental, emotional, physical and financial destiny*. London, United Kingdom: Simon & Schuster.

Effect of hunger on decision-making

DeAngelis, M., and profile, V. my complete (2010) *Legal Studies classroom*. Available at: http://legalstudiesclassroom.blogspot.co.uk/2011/04/legal-realism-justice-is-best-served-on.html (Accessed: 20 August 2016).

Appelbaum, B. (2011) *Up for parole? Better hope you're First on the docket*. Available at: http://economix.blogs.nytimes.com/2011/04/14/time-and-judgment/?_r=0 (Accessed: 20 August 2016).

Delaying gratification

Mischel, W. (2014) *The marshmallow test: Mastering self-control*. United States: Little, Brown, and Company.

Harnessing The Power Of Emotional Management

Whatever doesn't kill you makes you stronger and more emotionally resilient

Taleb, N.N. (2013) *Antifragile: How to live in a world we don't understand*. London: Penguin Books.

Traf-O-Data story

Balasa, V. (2007) *Failure is feedback: How 5 Billionaires had to fail to succeed*. Available at: http://www.hongkiat.com/blog/fail-to-succeed-billionaires/ (Accessed: 20 August 2016).

Anthony Robbins story

CNN(Producer).(2001, January 7). Tony Robbins: Practicing What He Preaches [TRANSCRIPT]. Retrieved from http://transcripts.cnn.com/TRANSCRIPTS/0101/07/pin.oo.html

Acceptance- Learning to accept what you can't accept

Branden, N. (1995) *The six pillars of self-esteem*. New York, NY: Random House Publishing Group.

Belly Breathing Exercise

David (2009) *A breathing exercise that calms panic attacks*. Available at: http://www.anxietycoach.com/breathingexercise.html (Accessed: 20 August 2016).

Facial feedback hypothesis

(No Date) Available at: http://wexler.free.fr/library/files/strack%20(1988)%20inhibiting%20and%20facilitating%20conditions%20of%20the%20human%20smile.%20a%20nonobtrusive%20test%20of%20the%20facial%20feedback%20hypothesis.pdf (Accessed: 20 August 2016).

Asking beneficial questions and changing sub-modalities

Robbins and Robbins, A. (1992) *Awaken the Giant within How to take immediate control of your mental, emotional, physical and financial destiny*. London, United Kingdom: Simon & Schuster.

Developing self-discipline

Duhigg, C. (2012) *The power of Habit: Why we do what we do in life and business*. New York: Random House Publishing Group.

Quinn, E. (2016) *Visualization, and mental rehearsal can improve athletic performance*. Available at: https://www.verywell.com/visualization-techniques-for-athletes-3119438 (Accessed: 20 August 2016).

Living by principles and integrity and effective criticism

Branden, N. (1995) *The six pillars of self-esteem*. New York, NY: Random House Publishing Group.

Learning How To Read People And Grasping Social Awareness

Social Awareness definition

Dgadmin (2015) *Daniel Goleman: How emotionally intelligent are you?* Available at: http://www.danielgoleman.info/daniel-goleman-how-emotionally-intelligent-are-you/ (Accessed: 20 August 2016).

Bill Clinton Presence

*, N. (2015) *Learn charisma from Bill Clinton in three steps. | immigrant entrepreneur.* Available at: http://www.immigrant-entrepreneur.org/tipps-und-tricks/learn-charisma-from-bill-clinton-in-three-steps.html (Accessed: 20 August 2016).

Relationship Management

Basing relationships on win/win

Covey, S.R. (2004) *The 7 habits of highly effective people: Powerful lessons in personal change.* New York: Simon & Schuster Adult Publishing Group.

Conflict negotiation

Conflict resolution (2011) Available at http://www.skillsyouneed.com/ips/conflict-resolution.html (Accessed: 20 August 2016).

Verbal Judo

Thompson, G.J., and Jenkins, J.B. (2014) *Verbal Judo: The Gentle art of persuasion.* New York, NY, United States: HarperCollins.

Story about George's son

Columbia Business School (2009) *Verbal Judo: Diffusing conflict through conversation.* Available at: https://www.youtube.com/watch?v=btBw70HAys4 (Accessed: 20 August 2016).

The effects of being nice instead of kind of relationships

Glover, R.A. (2003) *No more Mr. Nice guy.* Boston, MA, United States: Recorded Books.

Allais, M and O. Hagen, eds. 1979. Expected Utility Hypothesis and the Allais Paradox. Hingham, MA:D. Reidel

Baron, R. A. 1988 Negative effects of destructive criticism: Impact On Conflict, self-efficacy and task performance. Journal of Applied Psychology, Vol 73(2)

Branden, N., and Br, N. (1994) *The six pillars of self-esteem*. New York, NY: Bantam Dell Pub Group (Trd).

Berthoz, A. and Weiss, G. (2006) *Emotion and reason: The Cognitive Neuroscience of decision making*. Oxford: Oxford University Press.

Charles, H. H., and E.V. Clark. 1977. Psychology and language. New York: Harcourt.

Covey, S.R. (2004) *The 7 habits of highly effective people: Powerful lessons in personal change*. New York: Simon & Schuster Adult Publishing Group.

Dallek, R. (1999) *Flawed Giant: Lyndon Johnson and his times, 1961-1973*. New York: Oxford University Press, USA.

Dimitrius, J. 2008. Reading People. Ballantine Books

Erickson, D.K., Indiana University, B. and Kelley School of Business. Accounting and Information Systems Department. (no date) *How affect influences investors' effort to process financial information*.

Fishburn, P. C., and G.A. Kochenberger. 1979 "Two-Piece von Neumann-Morgenstern Utility functions."

Kahneman, D. 2011. Thinking Fast and Slow. London. Penguin Group

Lenski, T. (2014) *The conflict Pivot: Turning conflict into a peace of mind*. United States: Myriaccordmedia.

Lincoln, R. and Photographer, H.S. (2012) *Decoding keys to a healthy life*. Available at: http://news.harvard.edu/gazette/story/2012/02/decoding-keys-to-a-healthy-life/ (Accessed: 1 August 2016).

Hogg, T. (2002) *Blackwell handbook of social psychology: Group processes.* Edited by Michael A. Hogg and Scott Tindale. Malden, MA: Blackwell Publishing.

Mischel, W. (2014) *The marshmallow test: Mastering self-control.* United States: Little, Brown, and Company.

Nicholls, A.R., and Jones, L. (2012) *Psychology in sports coaching: Theory and practice.* New York: Routledge.

(No Date) Available at: https://scholar.harvard.edu/files/jenniferlerner/files/annual_review_manuscript_june_16_final.final_.pdf (Accessed: 1 August 2016).

Savage, L. J. 1954. The foundation of statistics. New York: Wiley

Slovic, P., B. Fischhoff, and S. Litchenstein.1982."Response Mode, Framing, and information-Processing Effects in Risk Assesment." in New Directions for Methodology of Social and Behavioral Science: Question framing and response consistency, ed. R. Hogarth. San Francisco: Josey-Bass.

Robbins, A. 1991. Awaken The Giant Within: How To Take Immediate Control Of Your Mental, Emotional, Physical And Financial Destiny. New York, NY: Free Press

Syed, M. 2010. Bounce. London: Fourth Estate

Taleb, N. 2012. Antifragile. London Penguin

Thomson, G. Verbal Judo: The Gentle Art Of Persuasion. New York: Harper Collins